The Grizzly Bear Hotshots

by **Kathleen Carey**

illustrated by **Ben Shannon**

Scott Foresman
is an imprint of

PEARSON

Glenview, Illinois • Boston, Massachusetts • Chandler, Arizona
Upper Saddle River, New Jersey

Illustrations
Ben Shannon

Photographs
Every effort has been made to secure permission and provide appropriate credit for photographic material. The publisher deeply regrets any omission and pledges to correct errors called to its attention in subsequent editions.

Unless otherwise acknowledged, all photographs are the property of Pearson Education, Inc.

24 © Peter Dasilva/epa/Corbis

ISBN 13: 978-0-328-51672-8
ISBN 10:   0-328-51672-4

4 5 6 7 8 9 10 V0FL 14 13 12 11

My uncle and I gazed out at what seemed like a million miles of forestland. We were standing on the deck of a high lookout tower in the middle of the dense woods of Idaho's "panhandle"—that long, narrow, northern part of the state.

From the deck, you couldn't see any signs of human life. Instead, it was just woods, spreading out for miles in all directions. The thousands of trees made a wild green carpet that stretched up the mountainsides and dipped into the shadowy valleys far below.

It was a perfect morning, clear and breezy. The sun was beginning its climb into the sky, and the air had that sweet pine scent that made you feel sorry for people who spent their whole lives in the city. A golden eagle soared overhead. You probably wouldn't find those beautiful birds in the city, either.

In a way, I felt like that eagle. I was soaring too. I had been ever since I'd found out that I'd made the Grizzly Bear crew—a team of woodland firefighters known as "hotshots." Hotshots have a reputation for being some of the best woodland firefighters. I was supposed to start tomorrow and could hardly wait to get a chance to prove myself. I'd show everybody. I'd be the best of the best.

"I can't wait to fight the wildfires out here," I said to my uncle. "Those fiery beasts better watch out for me!"

"It's risky business, Joey," he said, looking serious. "Fighting a forest fire takes total dedication. So you be careful out there. You're the only nephew I've got."

"Ah, don't worry about me," I said confidently. "I'm a hotshot. And there aren't any better woodland firefighters!"

Uncle Deke knew all about being a hotshot. He'd been one himself when he was younger, working on the ground, up-close to the fire. There was no one stronger or braver than the hotshots. Uncle Deke had done it for eleven years. Now he was a top-notch forest ranger. He supervised the care and protection of the forest.

"I'm serious, Joey. It's essential that you don't get overly confident out there, that's all I'm saying."

"Come on, Uncle Deke," I said, "you must've been excited when you became a hotshot."

Uncle Deke looked at me for a long minute, then said, "You're right, son. But a hotshot never takes anything for granted. Fire is unpredictable, and you just never know what it might throw at you."

I was only nineteen, but I knew something about fire. You had to be at least eighteen to become a hotshot, and it was all I'd wanted since high school. I'd had to go through intensive training to get hired onto the crew, but I'd finally made it. Now I was itching for real-life experience.

I didn't care that the job meant sleeping only four or five hours a night and getting up at 4 a.m. when a fire was raging. Or that we might be out in the woods fighting a blaze for three weeks straight before we got a single day off. It almost didn't even bother me that I might have to wait as long as a week just to take a shower. The only thing that mattered was that—*finally*—I was a hotshot!

"You know I'm the youngest guy on the whole Grizzly Bear crew, right, Uncle Deke?" I grinned at the thought of it. "That's saying something, don't you think?"

Uncle Deke shrugged and laughed. "Sure is, Joey. And I know you'll do a good job. I'm proud of you, real proud." He looked up at the sky. "It's going to be another hot one, I'm afraid."

The weather had been hot, dry, and uncomfortable for days. I'd seen some lightning the night before, but not a drop of rain had fallen. When it came to the threat of forest fire, these were not great conditions. I was well aware of that. But I was glad my uncle was finally turning his attention to something other than the dangers of my new career.

"Have you found someone to be the new lookout?" I asked.

Deke nodded. "A poet. He just wants some solitude and a big dose of nature. He's coming in this afternoon. Let me go check the radio, then we'll get back down to the ranger station."

Uncle Deke left me on the deck to go inside the tower's living quarters and check the radio. It was critical that the radio was working. It was the only means of communication with the outside world and other towers.

After Uncle Deke had gone inside, I took a cruise around the deck to look at the view from all sides. I tried to imagine what it would be like to be a lookout, living alone up in a forest tower like this. As a lookout, my main task would be watching and waiting, keeping my eye out for the first sign of fire.

The lookout job attracts all kinds of individuals: moms, artists, and people who want to get away from big-city life. It is extremely important, but it is a job I definitely wouldn't want to do. The isolation and the quiet would be great for a day or two, but lookouts do it for months on end, even years. I would miss the action and the energy that is part of being around other people.

When I got to the opposite side of the tower, I spotted something I didn't like. A thin, gray streak, like a ghostly ribbon, was winding up out of the treetops in the far distance. Fire.

I scanned the sky. No planes were buzzing anywhere, as they might have been if someone already knew about the fire. A plane might be carrying someone just trying to locate the fire, or to see how far it had spread. Or it might be carrying smokejumpers, whose job it is to harness themselves into a parachute and jump down to the fire's edge from planes circling in the air. Usually, smokejumpers are called in early to try to keep a fire from spreading. The hotshots come in later.

I was still concentrating on the trail of smoke, trying to determine how bad it was, when Uncle Deke hustled out.

"Let's hit the road, Joey," he said. "They've got a wildfire north of here. The wind is really kicking it up."

"There it is, Uncle Deke," I said, pointing out the distant gray cloud. It was getting bigger already.

"Looks like you might be starting your new job sooner than you thought."

My uncle looked worried, but I felt a thrill go through my body. I was ready.

At the ranger station, Uncle Deke and I parted ways. I took off in my own truck for the Grizzly Bear camp. As I drove, I mentally reviewed every firefighting method I'd learned and practiced during my training. Our job was basically to keep the fire from moving in any direction. We had to contain it, steer it away from dead trees and other materials that would give it fuel.

To do this, we'd clear the land of those fuels and dig deep, wide trenches, or pits, right alongside the fire. I'd heard hotshots laughing, saying they worked with one foot in the green and one foot in the black–in other words, standing half in the fire and half on the ground that hadn't yet burned.

Hotshots don't use water to put out the fire. They only use hand tools, like chainsaws, axes, and pulaskis. The pulaski, which looks like a hoe on one end and an axe on the other, is one of the most useful tools for hacking away roots, brush, and other fuels in the fire's path. Of course, other firefighters use these tools too, but everyone says the hotshots do it better, faster, and in worse conditions than anybody else.

As I came around a bend, I saw the Grizzly Bear headquarters up ahead. I pulled in and immediately the crew leader came hustling toward me.

"Joe!" he said, as I got out. He quickly gave me an update on the fire and said, "I know it's sudden, but I need you. I'm sending you out with the crew right away."

Uncle Deke's prediction had been right, and I couldn't believe how lucky I was. Under normal circumstances, a new crew member would ease in slowly, and not be sent in to battle a fire right away. But things were far from normal. Because of the high winds, the fire was eating up the forest at a dangerous speed. The crew needed all the help they could get.

11

In minutes, I got my gear together, changed into my bright yellow uniform, and was on the road in one of the big trucks that said in large red letters "Grizzly Bear Hotshots." Unfamiliar faces surrounded me. They were friendly but mostly talked among themselves like longtime buddies.

But then a girl's voice called me by name. "Joe, do you think you're ready?" she asked.

I rolled my eyes. I hadn't noticed her when I'd gotten in the truck. I'd heard about some women who were hotshots, but it hadn't occurred to me that I might actually be working with one on my own crew. Later, I learned her name was Erin.

"I'm not worried," I said with a smile, then turned to the two guys seated closest to me. "We'll control the beast, no problem, right?"

"We always do, but it's not always easy," one replied, his face grim.

I could tell they didn't think I took my job seriously. Well, I did, and soon they'd see I knew exactly what I was doing.

As we drew closer to the source of the blaze, the sky darkened to an ashy gray. Smoke was filling the air and burning the inside of my nose. We parked the trucks and started hiking in. Erin was up ahead and, I noticed, carrying a pack as large as any of the guys'. I was impressed and wondered how she would do.

But I couldn't think about that now. We had entered a monstrous, hazy world where an eerie red light danced and flickered all around us. And as we got closer, the crackling sound of burning timber began to increase to a deafening roar. The heat was intense too. We were rushing into a flaming furnace, frantically trying to clear the underbrush as we went.

Suddenly, there we were, truly right on the edge of it. The beast screamed with a thousand fiery tongues as the whole crew began digging and clearing with tremendous speed. Two guys with chainsaws were working on trees in the fire's path. Others were running down the slope with their tools, hoping to get a jump on the fire's course.

People were shouting at one another too. The crew leader was hollering commands, but it all seemed distant to me now. I was digging wildly along with the rest, but the voices had faded to nothing but faint, confusing noise behind the fire's tremendous roar. There was only that and the horrible pounding of my heart.

The land was steep and rocky, and the fire was smoking heavily. I could see it was burning fiercely, too, and spreading fast. I gasped for air, but kept hacking and digging.

Then all at once, a strong wind surged around me. The fire screamed and howled. A new patch of forest exploded into flames that climbed to fifty feet in only seconds. I watched as two tall pines became pillars of fire. I broke from the line and ran uphill, thinking I could start digging a new trench higher up to keep the fire from spreading sideways.

Behind me, another flaming tree crashed to the ground, sending sparks in all directions. The wind was a tremendous force that unexpectedly shifted and turned. Without warning, the wind was now carrying the fire back up the steep grade of the mountain.

Suddenly, fear clogged my throat. Every woodland firefighter knows that fire burning upward moves much faster than fire moving downward. And I was now in the fire's direct path, cut off from the rest of my crew. I didn't have any idea how it had happened, but I instantly saw the danger I was in. I was almost completely surrounded by flames. In other words, I was a goner.

Overcome by smoke and heat and fear, I sunk to my knees. I was dizzy and my vision was blurry. But at the back of my mind, something was nagging at me. It was telling me to get out my "shake and bake." That's what hotshots jokingly call the fireproof tents they each carry with them. My training had taught me that when a fire was coming at you and there seemed to be no way out, you crawl in there and wait it out. In a bad situation, it could be your only hope.

I clawed at my gear, trying to pull the tent free. Finally I got hold of it, but the fire was exploding in my ears. My oxygen was gone. Burning bits of wood were flying in all directions around me. I struggled to get the tent open. But all at once, everything went dark and silent.

The next thing I remember was the roar of fire coming back to my ears. The blood-red light returned. Someone had grabbed my jacket and was pulling me up to a seated position. I heard someone screaming at me to stand.

I tried to clear my head and struggled to find my footing. The smoke was still smothering me, but I managed to get up. I stumbled in confusion, but strong hands had a good hold on me, and I let them lead me.

As we made our way forward, the air began to clear slightly. Still having trouble breathing, I kept my head down. I saw we were walking on black, charred ground, and I understood what that meant. The crew had lit a backburn—they had purposely set fire to an unburned area so that it wouldn't fuel the big fire. A backburn ordinarily burned out quickly, stopping the oncoming blaze. It was an important method for containing woodland fires.

That scorched ground was important to me too, I saw. The path it created allowed my crew to get to me; it also provided a safe exit.

I wiped my blackened face, and looked up to see which of my guys had saved me. The second our eyes connected, though, I felt a jolt of shocked surprise. Two bright blue eyes, full of concern, were staring back at me from another sooty face. It was not a guy who had rescued me. It was Erin.

I shook my head and laughed at myself; I couldn't help it.

"Erin?" I said, disbelieving. "I don't believe it!" Then, in a low voice, I added, "Thanks."

Erin half-smiled. "First fire is always the worst," she said. "Hanging close to the rest of the crew isn't a bad idea, you know?"

What could I say? Erin was right. I'd taken off up the mountain thinking I could save the day by starting a new trench. But being a hotshot meant sticking to the rules and following orders from the team leaders. That's how everyone survives.

Seeing that I was alright, the rest of the crew cheered. I was better than alright, I realized. I was alive! I was doing the job I'd always wanted. And I'd learned an important lesson on my first day.

I also realized that being a hotshot meant more than showing off, it was a big responsibility—one that deserved respect. I would have to earn the respect of everyone on my crew, especially Erin. Just like she'd earned mine.

Real-Life Hotshots

Hotshot crews work for the U.S. Forest Service and other government agencies, and not just at fires close to their home base. In emergencies, they may be sent anywhere a fire is raging out of control—even as far away as Canada or Mexico.

America's hotshot crews are often referred to as the elite among woodland firefighters. They're sent into the most dangerous, hard-to-get-to, and hottest areas of a fire. And woodland fires can be scorching—sometimes reaching temperatures of up to 2,500 degrees. In fact, being in these intense hot spots is exactly why the crews are called "hotshots."

Being a hotshot takes courage, discipline, and intensive training. The fitness requirements, for both men and women, include being able to run one and a half miles in ten and a half minutes and hiking three miles in forty-five minutes while carrying forty-five pounds!